EATING WORMS

Practicing Leadership Every Day

Karen A. Snyder, MS, CSP, ICF

Introduction

You might be wondering what worms are doing on the cover of a leadership book. I think about worms each time I notice that voice in my head chattering about how things "should be." I know you have a voice in your head too. When I feel frustrated that something doesn't seem right, or fair, or I am I upset, I think of the children's song that is written below. In fact, not only do I think about the song, the lyrics get stuck in my head.

Allow me to share the lyrics with you, so they can get stuck in your head too:

> *Nobody likes me, everybody hates me,*
> *I think I'll go eat worms!*
> *Big fat juicy ones*
> *Eensie weensy squeensy ones*
> *See how they wiggle and squirm!*

To be fair, until I started writing this book, the only lyrics I knew were the first two lines. "Nobody likes me, everybody hates me. I think I'll go eat worms!" When my kids would whine to me, and I was tired of being empathetic, I would sometimes retort, "Maybe you should go out and eat worms." Fortunately, I have not ever told a client to consider eating worms.

A zillion times a day, well, to be clear, I have never actually counted, we have a choice about how we will respond to everyday situations. How will we respond to people who are annoying? How will we respond to policies that don't make sense? Will we shift and choose to respond or will we be stuck in the unfairness of life? Will we go out and eat worms?

I found that most of my blogs sort of "took on" the question of whether to shift our mindset or not. This book is a compilation of some of my readers' favorite blogs. With each blog are thought questions so you can consider the message and how it appears in your own life. I hope you will read the blogs, not necessarily in order, and use the questions to ponder.

I hope that the book will help you realize that leadership is not a title or a position, it is a way of living, a way of working, and a way of thinking. All of us have choices, all day, everyday, about how we will respond to situations. May you respond as a leader, much more often than not, and when you do respond less than perfectly, be forgiving of yourself. You will do better next time!

At the end of each chapter there are questions to stimulate 'the inner leader' within in you. Read, enjoy, and don't eat worms.

Table of Topics

Active Listening

Pay No Attention to the Pink Elephant 13

The More Specific, The More Terrific 29

Drinking and Driving in Cubicles 41

Fruit Loops 51

Are You Using the Right Signs? 65

Behaviors

You Are What You Eat 1

Mirror Mirror on the Wall 5

Positive Outcomes 17

Self-Defeating Behaviors 37

Drinking and Driving in Cubicles 41

We're All Funny 47

Luck Surface Area 85

Challenges

You Are What You Eat 1

Explain, Don't Complain 9

Positive Outcomes 17

Self-Defeating Behaviors 37

We're All Funny 47

Who Are We Protecting? 55

Wired 63

Teach Your Kids to Ask for the Ketchup 73

Luck Surface Area 85

Communication

Explain, Don't Complain 9

Pay No Attention to the Pink Elephant......................................13

I Like the Way You Part Your Hair 21

Rule Rethinking...25

Bullying in the Workplace..33

Self-Defeating Behaviors 37

Drinking and Driving in Cubicles...41

We're All Funny 47

Fruit Loops 51

Who Are We Protecting? 55

How A Spider Taught Me to Be More Sensitive 59

Wired...63

Are You Using the Right Signs?..65

Teach Your Kids to Ask for the Ketchup..................................73

Good Cop, Bad Cop: A Lesson for Leaders...............................77

Tape and WD-40 81

Conflict Resolution

Rule Rethinking...25

The More Specific, The More Terrific 29

Bullying in the Workplace..33

Self-Defeating Behaviors 37

How A Spider Taught Me to Be More Sensitive 59

Difficult Conversations

Explain, Don't Complain 9

I Like the Way You Part Your Hair 21

Who Are We Protecting? 55

How A Spider Taught Me to Be More Sensitive 59

Diversity and Inclusion

Self-Defeating Behaviors 37

Fruit Loops 51

How A Spider Taught Me to Be More Sensitive 59

Feedback and Recognition

Explain, Don't Complain 9

The More Specific, The More Terrific 29

Who Are We Protecting? 55

Friday Night Football 69

Life Lessons

You Are What You Eat 1

Explain, Don't Complain 9

Pay No Attention to the Pink Elephant 13

Positive Outcomes 17

I Like the Way You Part Your Hair 21

Drinking and Driving in Cubicles 41

Fruit Loops 51

Who Are We Protecting? 55

How A Spider Taught Me to Be More Sensitive 59

Are You Using the Right Signs? 65

Teach Your Kids to Ask for the Ketchup 73

Tape and WD-40 81

Meetings

Explain, Don't Complain 9

Wired...63

Tape and WD-40 81

Mindset

You Are What You Eat 1

Mirror Mirror on the Wall 5

Pay No Attention to the Pink Elephant............................13

Positive Outcomes..17

I Like the Way You Part Your Hair 21

Rule Rethinking..25

Self-Defeating Behaviors 37

We're All Funny 47

Fruit Loops 51

How A Spider Taught Me to Be More Sensitive 59

Are You Using the Right Signs?.......................................65

Teach Your Kids to Ask for the Ketchup...........................73

Good Cop, Bad Cop: A Lesson for Leaders.......................77

Luck Surface Area 85

Morale

Mirror Mirror on the Wall...5

Positive Outcomes..17

I Like the Way You Part Your Hair 21

Self-Defeating Behaviors...37

Fruit Loops 51

Luck Surface Area 85

Motivation

You Are What You Eat 1

Mirror Mirror on the Wall 5

Positive Outcomes 17

Who Are We Protecting? 55

Wired 63

Teach Your Kids to Ask for the Ketchup 73

Performance Management

Are You Using the Right Signs? 65

Good Cop, Bad Cop: A Lesson for Leaders 77

Perspective

Mirror Mirror on the Wall 5

Pay No Attention to the Pink Elephant 13

Positive Outcomes 17

I Like the Way You Part Your Hair 21

Rule Rethinking 25

The More Specific, The More Terrific 29

Drinking and Driving in Cubicles 41

We're All Funny 47

Who Are We Protecting? 55

How A Spider Taught Me to Be More Sensitive 59

Wired 63

Are You Using the Right Signs? 65

Teach Your Kids to Ask for the Ketchup 73

Good Cop, Bad Cop: A Lesson for Leaders 77

Positivity

You Are What You Eat 1

Mirror Mirror on the Wall 5

Explain, Don't Complain 9

Positive Outcomes... 17

We're All Funny 47

Fruit Loops 51

How A Spider Taught Me to Be More Sensitive 59

Friday Night Football... 69

Teach Your Kids to Ask for the Ketchup 73

Good Cop, Bad Cop: A Lesson for Leaders 77

Luck Surface Area 85

Respect

Mirror Mirror on the Wall 5

Explain, Don't Complain 9

Rule Rethinking... 25

The More Specific, The More Terrific 29

Bullying in the Workplace... 33

Self-Defeating Behaviors... 37

Fruit Loops 51

Who Are We Protecting? 55

How A Spider Taught Me to Be More Sensitive 59

Good Cop, Bad Cop: A Lesson for Leaders 77

Tape and WD-40 81

Team Building

Rule Rethinking..25

The More Specific, The More Terrific 29

Self-Defeating Behaviors 37

Fruit Loops 51

Friday Night Football..69

Workplace Culture

Explain, Don't Complain 9

Pay No Attention to the Pink Elephant...............................13

Rule Rethinking..25

Bullying in the Workplace..33

Self-Defeating Behaviors 37

Fruit Loops 51

Who Are We Protecting? 55

How A Spider Taught Me to Be More Sensitive 59

Wired..63

Are You Using the Right Signs?...65

Friday Night Football..69

Good Cop, Bad Cop: A Lesson for Leaders.......................77

Tape and WD-40 81

Chapter I

You Are What You Eat

Remember that old saying "You Are What You Eat"?

I do. I remember posters in the school cafeteria, ads in magazines, and a lot of chortled high-school jokes, most of them in good fun.

"Don't be a grouch. What'd you eat for breakfast, anyway -- prickly pears?"

We got the message.

My colleagues in the National Speakers Association put a different twist on this concept. Ron says, "You are what you do, not what you talk about doing." Chris says, "Talking about writing isn't writing. Writing is writing."

I get those messages, too. So much so that I have a saying posted in my house that says, "Life is not a dress rehearsal."

When I hear people talk about taking a class, or learning to knit, or improving their professional skills, I think it's great! They have made a proclamation. What is even better is when they take their first real step.

A client told me that he wants his department to work more collaboratively. He told me that they work in silos, each doing their own thing. I asked him, "What's your plan?" He chuckled and said, "My plan was to call you and have YOU figure it out."

Recently, my friend told me that she intends to run a marathon in May. Even though she is currently running just a few miles a day, taking the first steps (literally) builds momentum. When she showed me her running plan, I believed she would do it. More importantly, she believes she will do it. And regardless of when or if this marathon occurs, she is getting more fit and more determined each day.

Let me invite you to consider, whether your goal is an individual goal or a group goal, whether you set your own milestones or work with a partner, that you are what you act on. You are what you eat. Your intentions aren't you, your actions are you.

I am thrilled that someone I coach is starting a new business; he's been talking about it for years. He put together a business plan and he opened a business checking account. He is diligently working on a website. How fabulous!

Our lives aren't happening somewhere else, or at some other time. We aren't the people we are going to become -- we're the people we currently are. Living in the present means doing what we believe in, now.

How do you create peace and calmness in your life?

_____

_____

_____

_____

_____

Do you have a daily practice for finding gratitude, peace, and/or stillness?

_____

_____

_____

_____

_____

Chapter 2

Mirror, Mirror, On the Wall

There is only one person in the world you can control. And you know who that person is!! Go look in the mirror! And while you're there, give yourself a thumbs up.

It's not easy to bring your best self to work everyday -- but you do. OK... maybe not last Friday, but who's counting? Do you take time to truly appreciate all you accomplish throughout the day? That's why I'm a big proponent of the concept of self-management: Being your own boss even when your paycheck is cut by someone else.

But self-management requires a shift in attitude, an acceptance that effective praise does not have to come from outside sources (even though it is nice when it does). You know when you've put in your best work -- and the effort it took to get it done.

So before you move on to your next task after filing that complex budget report, step back and acknowledge what you've achieved with a good old "Yay Me!" Maybe even take yourself out for a coffee. Not only will you notice a self-esteem boost, you might also see a surge in productivity, just like when you have a boss who is good at delivering positive feedback.

And do you appreciate yourself when a colleague says something snarky, and you choose to hold your tongue? Or when you see something really inappropriate, and you find just the right time and place to address it one-on-one? Or, for those of you who have trouble speaking up, do you silently applaud yourself when you pitch an idea at the meeting? We need to appreciate both our tangible work efforts AND the way we notice and manage our emotions and interactions.

While it's true that you are the only one you can control, it's also true that your opinion of you has a huge impact on your ability to succeed. So look within, and be the best manager you've ever had!

1. What tangible work product have you completed this week that deserves acknowledgement?

_____

_____

_____

_____

_____

2. Can you think of a time this week when you were proud of how you handled a situation?

_____

_____

_____

_____

_____

Chapter 3

Explain, Don't Complain...

My husband and I had the pleasure of taking our daughter, Katie, on college tours. The campuses were lovely with both young adults and spring flowers sprouting and growing.

And yes, we are one of those families that actually sits through the tours and listens to their advice. One of the admissions deans shared that admissions officers desire grades improving during the high school years in an upward trajectory, though sometimes that is not the case. He continued, telling the students, if your grades take a dip, just tell us "why." He said that the students may have had a long illness or perhaps their parents divorced, or a beloved grandparent died...any number of things could have happened that the admissions team would want to know. He continued by saying, "Explain, but don't complain.

That applies to many of my coaching clients, I thought. They need to "Explain, but not complain." Sometimes my clients feel puzzled about what to do when a project they are working on is over budget, or won't be completed by the deadline. They realize the problem, but they don't want to tell their superiors "just yet." They put off reporting for months, the problem continues to worsen, and when their superiors learn about it, they are furious.

Other clients are unsure about what to say when a colleague, or two or even three, aren't pulling their weight.

As a responsible employee, it's imperative to let colleagues, and especially superiors, know when things are going awry. It's not a matter of "if" they should be told, but more a matter of "how." That's when "explain, but don't complain" is so valuable. Practicing explaining the situation without even a hint of complaint is what will make you a shining star in your work place. It's how high school seniors are being taught to write and it's valuable at work too.

My very first manager at Bay State Junior College used to say, "Come with the problem and at least one solution." So, that would be "explain, don't complain, and then problem solve"… but that's not nearly as catchy.

1. In your day to day life, how do you shift from complaining to a more positive mindset?

_____

_____

_____

_____

_____

2. When you are talking with a complainer, how do you help them shift?

_____

_____

_____

_____

_____

Chapter 4

Pay No Attention to the Pink Elephant

At a recent retreat of senior-level managers, we started the day with a yoga session. What a positive way to open a meeting, don't you think?

The instructor arrived early, set up the room, and greeted the participants as we entered. We were doing the initial breathing exercises when she said, "Forget about all the emails piling up in your inbox. If you're worried about what might happen later in the retreat, let that go."

Her intention was exactly the opposite of the outcome! When we tell our minds what not to think about, that's pretty much all we can think about. The experience reminded me of a coach that I had who was keen on neuro-linguistic programming. This coach often says wittily, "Forget about the big pink elephant with white spots." Well, of course, what do you imagine we think about whenever she says this? Did you picture a pink elephant with white spots, just from reading this? It's impossible not to think about what's being described, even if only for a split second.

This is a valuable lesson for coaching employees and for improving performance. Rather than telling employees what not to do, tell them what to do. For example, instead of saying, "Don't turn in the report late again," ask, "How will you meet the March 15 deadline?" Instead of saying, "Don't be cranky with the customers," say, "Think what this customer means to our business and greet her with a smile."

It's a small adjustment, yet it will reap elephant-sized results.

1. When have you noticed people telling you what not to do?

_____

_____

_____

_____

_____

2. When have you told others what not to do?

_____

_____

_____

_____

_____

Chapter 5

Positive Outcomes

Many years ago, I was at a networking event (with my four-month-old daughter strapped into a snuggly), and I was lamenting to some colleagues that the lion's share of my consulting business came from one client - a great client with whom I thoroughly enjoyed working, but one client nonetheless. I feared that I was not creating the stability I needed to build a successful business. If that one client pulled out, I'd be sunk, I griped.

This reaction from a colleague made a huge impact on my business acumen. "Let me get this straight," said Corrine. "You have a client you love, you have three children who are healthy, and you're worried? You should be grateful."

I left that event thinking: She is right. My cup is way beyond half full. I need to focus on what I have, instead of what I don't have.

Positivity is a powerful business tool. And while the field of positive psychology offers up a bevy of evidence for the connection behind optimism and positive outcomes, my belief in the concept came from a personal experience.

I was reminded of a networking event when a coaching client told me, "I am just going to pour positive energy into what's in front of me! Not because it's something I should do, but because when I pour positivity into anything, it seems to get better."

All of us can learn from this. In organizations, we tend to focus on what is going wrong instead of what is going right. And when we fail to pay attention to what's going right, it can evaporate pretty quickly.

Sometimes it takes a lot of effort to reframe your mindset. Let's say that your team landed three new clients, but missed their revenue goal. The negative message is that the team failed. The positive message is that any of those three clients have the potential to become million-dollar clients.

Or maybe your logo redesign required lots of back and forth with the design team. Negative message: This costs more than we planned. Positive message: We ended up with a logo that everyone is happy with and that will endure.

So how can you inject your workplace with positivity?

1. What have I done well this week?

_____

_____

_____

_____

_____

2. Whose work in the last month should I affirm with praise or a
    note of recognition?

_____

_____

_____

_____

_____

3. Even if I'm not the manager, how will I reward team members
    who have contributed to our success this quarter?

Chapter 6

_____

_____

_____

_____

_____

I Like the Way You Part Your Hair

When my son was in the second grade, I volunteered in his class. It was a classroom with eight very gifted, yet very challenging, young boys. One particular afternoon, one of the little boys in the class was particularly cranky and angry. I asked the teacher, "How do you reach him?" And she said, "It's easy. I just give him a genuine compliment." I replied, "How do you do that on a day like today? He hasn't done anything to compliment." And she said, "I come up with something, even if it's just, 'I like your t-shirt,' or 'I like the way you part your hair.'" Incredulous, I repeated that to her, "I like the way you part your hair?!" "Yes, on the days he's so upset, so angry, so downtrodden, on those days he'll accept any compliment. He's so hungry for someone to notice something positive about him, to throw him a bone, even saying, 'I like the way you part your hair' is helpful to him."

Wow. I found this amazing, and I gave it a try. I looked for big, important things that he and the other students were doing, but when I couldn't find any, I would say something simple like, "I'm glad you're thinking about the assignment. I can see the wheels are turning in your head." Or, "You have your paper out. That's the first step."

I find this strategy to be true in my work life as well. Sometimes it's really difficult for me to find something positive to say to some of the people I have been hired to coach. They don't want to be there. They don't want coaching. They never signed up for it. They're not really motivated by the possibility of growth. In these moments, I say the simplest things, the most obvious things. "Thank you for showing up. Thank you for giving it a try. Thank you for considering what I'm saying."

Unfortunately, the negative stuff takes up more of our time and our energy. But when we focus on the positive, the positives grow. Here are some things for you to notice:

- I like that you followed up.

- I like that you started the conversation.

- Thank you for drawing it to my attention.

- Thank you for doing the research that you've done.

- Thank you for telling me that you're going to need some help.

- Thank you for letting me know you need more time.

And if all else fails you can always resort to, "I like the way you part your hair." It will work for all but the bald ones.

1. What was a time when you were feeling great and someone made you feel even brighter from their feedback?

_____

_____

_____

_____

_____

2. What was a time when you were struggling and someone brightened your mood by noticing the positive?

_____

_____

_____

_____

_____

3. Who will you give positive feedback to today?

_____

_____

_____

_____

_____

Chapter 7

Rule Re-Thinking

Is it time to reassess your office rules?

When I was in my twenties I went to visit my girlfriend Anne at her parents' home on the Kilmarnock River. Once there, I found myself helping with their spring cleaning ritual, and a ritual it was! It included setting up their porch for outdoor summer relaxation. Down from the attic came bright chairs and tables, seat cushions, and a huge 1960s indoor-outdoor carpet. Trying to show initiative, I started to unroll it.

"Stop!" came a roar from their entire family. Startled, I froze. They explained, "We start unrolling from this corner, not that corner." "Why?" I asked. The answer: Because that is the way it had always been done.

Now Anne's family was loving and generous. They invited me to share their home and go out on their boat. They treated us to a crab feast and they lavished attention on us. They just had rules. Some made sense to me, and all made sense to them. I see the same phenomenon in many workplaces. Think about the rules that you have in your office. If you use the last of the paper in the copy machine, do you replace it or is it the job of the person who follows you? If the workday starts at 8:30, is it okay to arrive at 8:31 or even 8:51?

Of course we need rules, but problems arise when we don't communicate and assess them. So ask yourself, "Are office rules serving you or are they getting in the way?" If you're not sure, ask your colleagues -- they will be happy to tell you if your rules are in their way!

Once you figure out the keepers, communicate them clearly and without judgment. I find starting with "I would appreciate it if...," is a great way to get the conversation started.

Let me give you an example of a rule done right. In a workplace I frequent, there is a sign above the copier that reads, "Use the second tray and input this code, or the copier will jam." I appreciate that clarity. I don't want to be the one who jams the copier and creates a big hassle. And that is really the litmus test for good rules: Do they make the workplace a more efficient, friendly, and productive environment for everyone?

1. What are some of the rules in your workplace, written or unwritten?

   _____

   _____

   _____

   _____

   _____

2. For unwritten rules, how do you know that everyone is aware of them?

   _____

   _____

   _____

   _____

3. Are there rules that are consistently broken? Why do you think that happens?

   _____

   _____

   _____

   _____

   _____

Chapter 8

The More Specific, The More Terrific

You can't improve if you don't know what you're doing wrong. Makes sense, doesn't it? In reality, many of us complain about underachieving co-workers, but don't give them the type of feedback they need to do their jobs better.

Let me give you an example: When I was the training director for a regional bank, we worked with Carrie, our assistant. Carrie, was an efficiency wiz. Her grammar was impeccable and when she proofed a document, she not only made corrections (in red), she made stylistic suggestions (in yellow) that improved documents tremendously. Carrie handled the workload of six vice-presidents with time to spare, whereas our previous assistant had always been behind. She revamped our filing system (yes, they were paper files back then!), cross-referencing everything, without being asked.

You're thinking, "What a joy!" right? Wrong!

Within a few months, it became clear that no one liked Carrie. All six VPs were avoiding her, and she was being left out of meetings because no one wanted to deal with her.

Roger, one of the VPs, tried to give Carrie feedback. He told her that she was grumpy. "You would be grumpy too," she nearly screamed, "if you were up all night with a toddler, had to get up at 5:30am to get her to daycare, and your life was nothing more than drudgery!"

Well, that was the end of Roger giving her feedback.

We decided Carrie needed a performance improvement plan, but what would we write? She was so talented and efficient. My colleague, Laurel, said she would take Carrie on as her project and see how she could help.

Laurel asked what specifically Carrie did that annoyed us. What made her grumpy?

We weren't sure. We talked about it for a few minutes. Finally, Juan said, "I don't like that she grunts when I walk in each morning."

"I thought she only did that to me," Gary said. "I think it's because she's focused on what she's working on," said Bea.

Laurel scheduled a meeting with Carrie. Laurel said simply, "In the morning, when each person arrives, please look up from your work and say any polite version of good morning."

Carrie turned red. "It rarely is a good morning!" she exclaimed. "I don't want to stop what I'm doing. It's not in my job description."

Laurel responded calmly, "You are the first person your colleagues and our visitors see each day. It is important that we create a positive work environment. If you would like, we can modify your job description to include greeting your colleagues and visitors professionally."

The next morning, Carrie grumbled a greeting as people entered the office.

Many of us greeted her back and smiled. Each day her greeting seemed a tiny bit more sincere. At the next staff meeting, everyone mentioned the difference. Laurel said, "Next we will work on asking Carrie to keep us updated on her status on our projects."

Within a year, Carrie applied for a role as an entry-level consultant – a position that was a much better match for her considerable abilities. We were able to give her excellent recommendations and she got the job!

1. So what made the difference between Roger's and Laurel's approaches?

_____

_____

_____

_____

_____

2. How can you use direct feedback in your workplace? (Is there someone in your office who is awesome? How so? Someone lazy? What are the actual behaviors of laziness?)

_____

_____

_____

_____

_____

Chapter 9

Bullying in the Workplace

I had a new assignment: I was asked to coach Tracy. Tracy was by definition morbidly obese. She was experiencing extreme distress and anxiety because her colleagues - grown adults - teased and taunted her about her weight. When the culprits were questioned, each acknowledged the behavior occurred within the department, but they said, "It wasn't that bad," and "They [not we] were only joking," and even, "We just did it once."

Interesting! We might think bullying is an issue that goes away once we are out of elementary school. But my years as a workplace consultant tell me that this is definitely not the case. In some workplaces, it is overlooked when inappropriate jokes are told, when comments are made, and when whispering occurs.

Researchers have found that when employees are asked, "Does bullying exist in your workplace?" they answer "Yes." But, when the same researchers ask "Do you ever bully?" the answer is "No."

Who do you suppose is doing the bullying?

I asked Tracy's colleagues, "What do you do to stop the bullying?" They responded that it wasn't their job to stop it.

Not only do I disagree with their attitude, so does the law: If people are being bullied based on their gender, gender preference, ethnicity, religion, age, or as in this example weight/physique, your organization is at risk.

But not only that: The behavior isn't nice, and it leads to a toxic work environment.

So, what do you do if you see this behavior happening?

1. Change the subject.

2. Talk to the perpetrators privately: "I'm really uncomfortable when you do that. This is how your behavior affects me."

3. Express your expectations: "It's really important to me that we treat one another with respect and that we only talk about people's ideas as they relate to work."

If these strategies don't work, you must, by law, report the behavior to your manager and to human resources. If your concerns are not taken seriously, you need to contact the U.S. Equal Employment Opportunity Commission (https://www.eeoc.gov/) and ask them to research the situation.

Are you a manager who is struggling to create a positive work environment? The law - and human decency - dictate that everyone has the right to an emotionally, as well as physically, safe workplace.

1. Is there a situation you find yourself in routinely where bullying occurs?

    _____

    _____

    _____

    _____

    _____

2. What proactive measures can you take to prevent bullying?

    _____

    _____

    _____

    _____

Chapter 10

Self-Defeating Behaviors

Oftentimes, when working in or with a group, a member's individual needs interfere with the group's effectiveness. Whether you are leading the group or you are a member of the group, the group's effectiveness depends on the ability to notice, manage and redirect self-defeating behaviors. When personal goals, yours or other members, are too strong, they hamper the ability of the group to reach their common goal.

Below are some examples of different types of self-defeating behaviors:

- Dependency/Counter dependency: Unrealistically "leaning on" or resisting anyone in the group who represents authority. ("You're right, of course; whatever you say I will agree to." "I'm not sure you're competent enough to make that judgment." "Let's run it by Suzanne. Without her approval we might as well go home.")

- Fighting and Controlling: Asserting personal dominance; attempting to get one's way regardless of others. ("Allen will not stand for that; it is wrong, wrong, wrong!" "No one knows this area like I do.")

- Withdrawing: Trying to remove frustration or uncomfortable feelings by psychologically leaving the group, or by physical departure in rare cases. (Symptoms may be such things as doodling, leaning back in the chair, and staring at the wall, and of course, hiding behind technology by texting, emailing or surfing during a meeting.)

- Pairing: Seeking out one or two supporters and forming a subgroup; protecting and supporting one another. (Such as: communicating in whispers while the "opponent" is talking; building coalitions by texting during a meeting.)

1. What are the norms in your organization?

_____

_____

_____

_____

_____

2. What self-defeating behaviors have you exhibited?

_____

_____

_____

_____

3. How can you begin to change dysfunctional behaviors?

_____

_____

_____

_____

Chapter 11

Drinking and Driving in Cubicles

I was driving my daughter Katie when she was about six years old. Along the way -- with a facial expression that communicated "I am very upset" -- she exclaimed, "Why are you drinking that?"

It was true that in the afternoons, when I was feeling exhausted, I sometimes drank Coca-Cola. It would give me a much-needed boost to make it through the remainder of the day. It was hard juggling a career, three kids, and a busy household. I explained to Katie that although the sugared and caffeinated drink was not healthy, it was helpful so that I could drive safely. I felt guilty, but what else could I say?

I could tell that my answer didn't win her over. Since Katie was my third child, and since I work with employees who are often unhappy, I admit that I was accustomed to giving unsatisfactory answers. I didn't think much more about it.

A few days later, I brewed a cup of my favorite herbal tea, Bengal Spice, and savored the strong cinnamon aroma. I was looking forward to sipping it on the way to a client's office. Before backing out of the driveway, I carefully placed my 16-ounce white thermal mug in the cup holder and put on my seat belt.

Katie, from the backseat, piped up, "Why did you bring that in the car?"

It was rather full indeed, and perhaps I had made a mistake in not taking time to find a lid. After all, it was likely that some of it would spill, but with 16 ounces I would still have plenty to drink. Plus the car was getting older, and it was nothing that a Clorox wipe couldn't handle.

I told Katie that if it spilled, we had wipes and I would clean it up. In the meantime, I was enjoying the scent filling the car. Katie was not pleased with my response, and I was not pleased with her policing the condition of my car. She got out of the car and headed in to school with an attitude.

We didn't even make it a few days more when I got in the car with an open can of seltzer. This time, Katie, on the verge of tears blurted, "Mom! Why do you keep drinking and driving?"

Finally, a light bulb went off. "Angel," I said, "What have you been taught about drinking and driving?"

Katie shared with me that she had learned that drinking and driving causes accidents and lost lives. That was about all she knew as a six year old. I gave Katie a mini-lesson on alcohol and its effects. As you can imagine, we both felt great relief after our chat.

Clearly, Katie and I had been miscommunicating and upsetting one another for days. But it wasn't just because Katie was a young child that the miscommunication occurred. Miscommunication happens in offices, in meetings, in cubicles, all day, every day.

When coaching Paul, a senior leader in a government agency, he explained his version of a new department initiative. Paul saw it as a way to further develop his team, to challenge one of his star employees with a stretch assignment, and to uncover some personnel issues that were previously obscured. I left the meeting thinking it was a brilliant move for all concerned.

Within hours, I was working with the director, Sandy, whom the new initiative would impact most significantly. Sandy was furious! She was certain she was being "picked on" due to her lack of tenure with the agency and because she was an over-achiever. She felt that she was being given "the impossible team" to manage, and that her director did not want her to succeed because he hated women. She was headed straight to her EEO office to file a grievance, but luckily she ran into her friend Diane in the hall.

Diane truly was a good friend because after she validated Sandy's feelings, she encouraged her to stop and think before she went to EEO. Diane encouraged Sandy to wait a few days and calm down and then go back and talk to Paul and share her feelings. Sandy did that and Paul was willing to put his own agenda aside and listen. After a couple of talks and brainstorming sessions, the two decided that future white papers coming from that office would have her name on them listed as an author which would give her the recognition she deserved. It was a classic example of how communication, coupled with openness and brainstorming, can change perception.

Sometimes, employers and their employees have different intentions. Other times, it's simple miscommunication. Usually, it's a bit of both.

I can't say that I am proud of the way I brushed off Katie and her concerns all those years ago. In our work groups and in our families, when we can see that someone is upset, it serves us and our organizations well to take the time to probe and hear, really hear, th other points of view.

1. What are some funny times in your life when there have been misunderstandings?

_____

_____

_____

_____

_____

2. Who do you have frequent misunderstandings with?

_____

_____

_____

_____

_____

3. How do you handle those misunderstandings?

_____

_____

_____

_____

_____

Chapter 12

We're All Funny

Picture this, if you can:

You are eight-and-a-half months pregnant (I know this may be tough, and it's about to get tougher).

It's the last child you plan to have, so you don't want to buy a bunch of maternity stuff you don't expect to need again. But you're a business person, so you want to project a professional image.

You're getting ready for a meeting with two prospective clients. You pull on that last pair of salvaged pantyhose, thinking how glad you are you won't have to wear them again, and notice they're a little loose.

You arrive. The two men you're meeting walk toward you, and the three of you set off across the parking lot.

You feel those pantyhose slip. You'll have to hit the restroom as soon as you get to the restaurant, but hey, you're pregnant--they'll probably expect it.

Now they're down around your hips. You pick up the pace.

Now they're at your thighs. You're waddling a little, hoping to keep them from sliding farther down. But pregnant women often waddle, right?

Now they're just above your knees, and you feel like a holiday turkey, legs bound up in a rubber band. Your waddle becomes a mince.

What do you do?

I stopped, and said "Excuse me, gentlemen. Sometimes you have to lighten your load." Then I took one of them by the arm, stepped out of my shoes, and pulled off the pantyhose (now hovering around my shins).

We went on to the restaurant, and no one said another word about it.

Was I embarrassed? You bet. But not only did I get the job (so it wasn't fatal), but I learned once again that the biggest difference between humor and embarrassment is how we handle it. Humorists teach us that people who can laugh at themselves make others comfortable, and gain their respect.

Plus, it's more fun to laugh than to squirm in mortification--or pantyhose.

1. What does fear of embarrassment prevent you from trying?

_____

_____

_____

_____

_____

2. What embarrassing moments have you had this year?

_____

_____

_____

_____

3. What do you do when something embarrassing happens?

_____

_____

_____

_____

_____

Chapter 13

Fruit Loops

I still remember the first time I noticed fall. I must have been four or five years old. I was with my family driving through the Blue Ridge Mountains, and I, through some miracle (or, more likely, maternal intervention), was sitting by the door, nose pressed against the window.

"It looks just like a bowl of Fruit Loops," my brother Rick said.

"Why are the trees all different colors?" I asked. "Why are some of them still green? Why are there red ones and yellow ones and orange ones?"

My mother didn't go into detail about chlorophyll and day length. She just said, "The forest has lots of different kinds of trees, and when it gets colder and there's less sunshine, they all respond in different ways."

Another brother chimed in, "It's a good thing they're different, or fall would just look like Rice Krispies!"

Whenever I present a program about diversity, I remember that eye-opening drive in the mountains. People often equate diversity training with ethnic diversity in the workplace. That's profoundly important, and essential.

But I like to remember, and include in the discussion, that all kinds of diversity--different backgrounds, work styles, attitudes, and perspectives--improve an organization's ability to respond to change, and to meet the needs of their diverse customers. Just like trees, people come in different kinds, and respond differently to their environment.

So look around you. Do you see Fruit Loops, or Rice Krispies?

1. In your personal life, who do you tend to socialize with? People who are like you or who are different from you?

_____

_____

_____

_____

_____

2. Is your organization proactive in attracting, hiring and retaining employees from varied backgrounds?

_____

_____

_____

_____

_____

3. How have you grown as a person from being around people who are different?

_____

_____

_____

_____

_____

Chapter 14

Who Are We Protecting?

One of my son's best friends was moving away. I knew it for months, but didn't tell him. I knew it would be hard for him, and I thought we should talk about it. But I also thought it would be better if he heard the news from his friend and came to me himself.

Weeks passed. All the adults in the neighborhood knew about the move, but my son still hadn't mentioned it. So, I decided I'd better tell him--if someone else hadn't already done it.

"Oh, yeah," was his response. "He told me last week. I wish he wasn't moving."

"I'm a little surprised you didn't talk to me about it," I said.

"I thought you didn't know," my son replied. "I thought you'd be hurt if you didn't hear it from the other moms."

Home isn't the only place where protecting people can backfire. It can happen at work, too.

The other day, one of my clients, very successful in her job, confided in me that she hadn't done so well with her previous company.

"What do you think makes the difference?" I asked.

"Good feedback," she said. "And I don't mean just positive feedback. My manager lets me know when I messed up, too. I got my feelings hurt a time or two, but I listened, and it paid off."

Are there things you aren't saying to people because you're afraid of hurting them or making them angry? Practice. Go to someone you trust, and role-play constructive ways to say what you need to say.

Then give someone the gift of direct, honest, tactful feedback.

1. Who are you protecting at work?

_____

_____

_____

_____

_____

2. Who are you protecting at home?

_____

_____

_____

_____

_____

3. In what ways does protecting others hurt relationships and trust?

_____

_____

_____

_____

_____

Chapter 15

How a Spider Taught Me to be More Sensitive

I conducted a "Positive Workplace" program for a large organization. I know what you might be thinking: "Ugh, another one of those programs" or "Isn't it enough that I work 50 hours a week? Do I have to be nice and 'positive' as well?"

I suspect the participants felt the same. I started off the program asking "How many people drive? How many people obey the speed limit ALL the time? How many people perceive the speed limit to be the speed limit plus 10 miles per hour over it?"

The point I was trying to make is that most of us consider ourselves to be law abiding and contributing members of society. And most of us also believe we are safe drivers. Yet, at one time or another, we violate the speed that is safest for ourselves and our fellow motorists, bicyclists and pedestrians. Likewise, while most of us perceive ourselves to be positive and productive colleagues, all of us need reminders.

Next, I asked if anyone had ever experienced a time when they felt that their values were being violated in the workplace. Up popped a hand, in record time.

Dorothy said, "Before I came here, in the place where I used to work, when a spider or an ant was on someone's desk, they killed it! They didn't take the time or effort to return it to nature. They just killed it! They killed one of God's creatures and they felt no remorse. I had to leave that place."

So, I have to admit, I am of the spider, ant and fly squashing camp. My only consideration is trying not to leave "bug juice" on the wall when swatting. It was an effort, a lot of effort, to hide my surprise.

But, through Dorothy's experience, I was reminded that each of us has different values and standards of what is appropriate at the workplace. Likewise, it's in everyone's best interest to create workplaces where differing values are respected.

When a colleague tells you that your jokes are offensive, your pranks feel like bullying or your music is too loud, find compassion, understanding and a middle ground. It takes courage to speak up and those that voice their needs deserve to be heard.

Yes, those that speak up need to be heard and we create better workplaces when we hear them.

1. What are your sensitivities?

    _____

    _____

    _____

    _____

    _____

2. When have you taken the time to explain your sensitivities?

    _____

    _____

    _____

    _____

    _____

3. What are other people sensitive about that has you rolling your eyes?

    _____

    _____

    _____

    _____

    _____

Chapter 16

Wired

had an appointment with a manager today.

She had a cell phone.

She had a desk phone with caller ID and three lines.

She wore a beeper.

During our 90 minutes together, each time a device rang or beeped, she responded. Although she responded to each of the 12 summonses in less than a minute, I left our meeting feeling jangled.

The next person I met with closed his office door as he came to greet me. He turned off the ringer on his phone, then looked up, and made eye contact. We covered our agenda. He took notes. We were not interrupted.

After 45 productive, business-focused minutes (and 10 minutes of chatting), I left feeling informed and connected.

1. Is it always responsible to be responsive?

_____

_____

_____

_____

_____

2. When are you wired instead of connected?

_____

_____

_____

_____

_____

3. What small steps can you take now to improve?

_____

_____

_____

_____

_____

4. How many hours do you spend each day without a device?

_____

_____

_____

Chapter 17

Are You Using the Right Signs?

One warm weekend this spring, we went to the beach.

My four-year-old daughter and I walked down the boardwalk.

We passed a new shop glowing with fresh white paint.

Vibrant red geraniums sat on windowsills framed in blue gingham curtains.

Through the doorway I could see sparking glass display cases and shiny clean tile.

A charming, hand-lettered sign read, "Candy of All Kinds--Come In."

"What a happy place," I thought as we passed by.

My daughter didn't give it a second glance.

She skipped along, swinging my hand.

A block later, she stopped and pointed. "Please, Mom. Please?"

In the middle of the next block, standing in the sidewalk, there was a four-foot ice cream cone--two pink scoops topped with a bright red cherry.

It was a sign that any child could understand.

She tugged my hand. "Please, Mom. Please?"

So we went in, and shared a cone. The table was smeared, the floor was unswept, and the display cases did not sparkle. But they knew what kind of sign to use.

1. Are you using the right signs to speak to your customers?

_____

_____

_____

_____

_____

2. What retail signs entice you?

_____

_____

_____

_____

3. What signs in your workplace help you to behave differently?

_____

_____

_____

_____

_____

Chapter 18

Friday Night Football

2-4-6-8

Who do we appreciate?

Team name, Team name, Team name...

You remember the cheer. You remember the thunderous applause at high school games.

I've always known how important appreciation is. I often do appreciation exercises in my programs and learn over and over again how effective and meaningful appreciation can be. I asked the participants to bring a gift (of little or no monetary value) affirming a colleague's strengths.

A law enforcement officer received a toy gun with a heart inside. This man had clearly shown that underneath his uniform and toughness was a caring man.

A woman who never takes lunch was presented with a lunch box to keep on her desk. Inside was an alarm clock, set for lunchtime, with this message: "Taking a break will increase your productivity. Enjoy!"

Another participant with a clear gift for mentoring employees was given a pretend tool box and Play Dough. The message said, "Thank for helping to mold our future leaders."

Genuine appreciation comes in all forms. A handshake. A hug. A thank you. A letter of praise. A symbolic gift. A chant at a ball game. The form doesn't matter. Genuine appreciation changes lives

If you appreciate someone, don't wait for an excuse to show it!

2, 4, 6, 8...

Who do you appreciate?

1. Is it important to show appreciation to people who act like they don't care? And if so, how do you show it?

_____

_____

_____

_____

_____

2. When have you shown your appreciation today?

_____

_____

_____

_____

_____

Chapter 19

Teach Your Kids to Ask for the Ketchup

Driving on a long car trip with my adult son Josh is always a pleasure. Josh's myriad of interests coupled with his loquaciousness makes for a pleasant journey. Travelling on Interstate 81, we were discussing pollution, global warming, poverty and the gravitational pull of the universe, to name just a few of the light topics.

Our discussion of poverty moved to income disparity, which led to salary inequality. Josh said that researchers have proven that employees who ask politely and professionally are granted more raises. Assuming that an employee asks once or twice a year, over a 40 year employment history, those increases of 1 to 2% can and do make a substantial difference.

Only half of the employed population has ever asked for a raise, according to PayScale.com.

We started discussing "If employees have this information, and they supposedly want more money, why don't they ask?"

At this point, my daughter Katie, who we thought was sleeping, piped up, "Because their parents don't teach them to ask for the ketchup."

"What?"

"Yeah, when I go out to dinner with friends, they don't ask for the ketchup. They won't even ask for a fork if they don't have one."

Katie continued, "They're so afraid that they won't be viewed as 'nice' that they won't even ask."

So, is asking for the ketchup a transferable skill? Are teenagers who can politely ask for the ketchup in a restaurant better equipped as young adults to ask for a raise? I think so and I am proud of Katie for seeing the correlation.

One of the questions I have for all of us is, do we consistently and appropriately ask for what we need and want in our work? If not, why not? If you don't feel comfortable in these situations, practice helps. If you're not teaching your children or your employees these skills, it's time to start.

And if you are one of those people who ask for the ketchup, the mustard, the mayonnaise, the relish, and the steak sauce, this chapter doesn't apply to you.

1. Are you asking politely for what you deserve in your professional life?

_____

_____

_____

_____

_____

2. Are you asking politely for what you deserve in your personal life?

_____

_____

_____

_____

_____

3. When you don't receive what you feel you deserve, what are polite and appropriate ways of asking again?

_____

_____

_____

_____

_____

Good Cop, Bad Cop: A Lesson for Leaders

At the risk of giving the impression that I'm a terrible driver, I would like to tell you about two very different encounters I have had with traffic officers. One afternoon after flying back from a presentation, I found my car in the parking lot and then I hit the road, excited to be going home. No sooner had I merged into traffic on the highway when I heard sirens behind me.

"Do you realize you went through a stop sign?" asked the officer. I did not. In fact, I had thought it was a yield sign, like most on-ramps. While I was contrite, I was also curious as to why this particular on-ramp was designed this way. The officer showed no interest in engaging in conversation and handed me a ticket for failure to stop.

Many months later, sirens blared after I turned into a neighborhood from a busy road. The officer approached my car, looked at my license, and peered into the backseat where my two young children looked wide-eyed back at him.

"Mrs. Snyder," he said firmly but empathetically, "I am concerned. You pulled very quickly into this neighborhood. You were exceeding the speed limit. What if you hit a child? It would ruin your life and the family of that child." That message hit home. Even though my kids are now adults, to this day, I always slow down when I enter a neighborhood. That officer's words still have an impact on me, these many years later.

Both of the officers used their power to pull me over, but only one used his influence to effect a positive, lasting change.

My question to you, as a leader, is this: Do you use your power effectively? Do you use your influence to effect a positive and lasting change?

When we fear someone, we do what they want us to do, quickly and in the moment - and when they are watching. But when we work with leaders who are influential and take the time and effort to connect with us, we take their direction to heart - even when they aren't watching.

In fact, being a leader is something like being a traffic officer. You keep a watchful eye and you pull people over when you are concerned about their behavior. It is what you do next that determines if your employee will incorporate your direction into their work habits, or simply comply in the moment because it's the path of least resistance.

If you're having difficulty achieving lasting compliance, maybe it's time to revisit your strategy.

1. In what ways at work are colleagues less compliant than you wish?

    _____

    _____

    _____

    _____

    _____

2. In what ways at home are family members less compliant than you wish?

    _____

    _____

    _____

    _____

3. What are some different strategies you could use to increase compliance even a little?

    _____

    _____

    _____

    _____

    _____

Chapter 21

Tape and WD-40

I was teaching a presentations skills workshop. Just as we were beginning the first break, someone new came in. "I couldn't sign up for this class," she said, "but I hope you'll help me anyway. I'm speaking at a conference next week. Do you have any quick suggestions for me?"

Well, I sure did. Here they are for you, too:

1. Use rope or ribbon and a sign to make a reserved section in the back of the room.

   You'll encourage people to sit closer to each other and to you. Who sits in the reserved section? People who arrive after you start speaking. Now they have a place to sit-- without being embarrassed, and without distracting the rest of the audience.

2. Manage cell phones, or they will manage you.

   One fun way is to ask participants to get out their cell phones and discover one feature they never use. Now ask them to find one of these features--off, no-ring, or vibrate.

(A word of caution: once a phone rings in the audience, it is very difficult to say anything that doesn't seem critical or condescending.)

3. Prepare for the unexpected.

    No presentation, speech, or facilitation ever happens exactly the way I expect. Most go smoothly, and leave me energized And often it's the unanticipated and unpredictable developments that make working with an audience fun.

4. Like sunsets and snowflakes, every audience is unique.

    Even if this group seems to be just like others you've worked with, be prepared for different reactions and feedback.

5. Don't try to be the expert. If you do, the audience will watch for your mistakes. If, on the other hand, you speak to them as a peer sharing your knowledge, they'll appreciate and support you-and share their knowledge.

6. If you relax, your audience will relax.

    More than likely, if you have fun, your audience will have fun. If you learn something, your audience will learn something.

7. And what about duct tape and WD-40?

    Make sure the door in the back of the room opens and closes quietly. Tape the latch. Sometimes little things make a big difference. No matter how engaging your presentation, someone may have to leave early.

Now your audience is seated close to you. Their cell phones are off. You are prepared for the unexpected, and attuned to this particular group. Everyone is sharing expertise. You're at least a little relaxed. When someone leaves early, you don't take it personally and no one else even notices.

So, pack up your duct tape and WD-40 and relax. Tape and WD-40!

1. In your business meetings, what can you do to change the room arrangement to be more conducive to the outcome you are trying to create?

_____

_____

_____

_____

_____

2. How do you manage your anxiety regarding 'being the expert'?

_____

_____

_____

_____

3. How do you calm yourself before meetings so others will be calm?

_____

_____

_____

_____

Chapter 22

Luck Surface Area

My son Josh taught my daughter Katie about Luck Surface Area. It is a concept coined by Jason Roberts from techzinglive.com.

Katie gave this example of Luck Surface Area. Imagine that every person begins life with a dartboard and one dart. Some of the dartboards are the size of a pin head, while others are the size of a football field. The dart is their luck, the board is the Luck Surface Area. The dart can only bring more good luck if it hits the dartboard. They go through life making choices, and if those choices are appropriate for the situation, their dartboard enlarges and of course the chance of the dart hitting the dartboard is greater. However the converse occurs when they make poor choices. When the person makes bad choices, the dartboard becomes so tiny that it seems like they are terribly unlucky and nothing good can ever happen for them.

I notice Luck Surface Area with the employees I coach. Many of the employees I consult are continuously exhibiting behaviors that increase their Luck Surface Area. They show up on time, they are generally positive, they share information, they seek and appreciate feedback. When these employees give critical feedback, they have solutions. They attack the problem, not the person. They meet their deadlines and when they can't, which is rare, there really are extenuating circumstances. All of these positive behaviors increase their Luck Surface Area at work.

1. How does the concept of Luck Surface Area show up in your life?

_____

_____

_____

_____

_____

2. When your Luck Surface Area is feeling small, how do you increase it?

_____

_____

_____

_____

_____

3. What are you doing to increase your Luck Surface Area?

_____

_____

_____

_____

_____

Acknowledgements

I want to thank Lane Goddard for helping me write my first newsletters back in the early nineties. I would go to her office and we would write together and it was a respite from my otherwise chaotic life. The newsletters were sent a few times a quarter. Over the years, the subjects have changed and the frequency increased, but without Lane, I never would have started writing.

More recently, I have Wanda DeShay, KimIrene Briggs and Wendy Culberson to thank for suggesting that I combine the blogs and put them into a book. Additionally, I want to thank each of them for being so encouraging in general. And how do you know if a person needs encouragement? If they are alive! My thanks to the three of you. Thanks to Jeri Mae Rowley for brainstorming glow worms, early birds getting the worms and a host of other wormie expressions. Jeri Mae, you are so creative and giving! And thank you to Ray Coyle, Debi Engle, Chris White, and Pat Williams. All of you are members of the frequent commenters club.

Readers, please note all the people who encouraged me. I think it takes hearing the same message more than once for the message to stick. Thus, I am either dense or we all need to encourage one another, you choose which one you wish to believe. I am glad those friends and colleagues repeated their message to me. I am incredibly thankful.

I want to thank Keri Christovich for keeping me organized. Well, she really doesn't keep me organized, she tries desperately to get me organized. And she never seems to eat worms regarding my disarray. And thanks to Mary Nixon for doing so much work behind the scenes to get the blogs out regularly. Mary is always compiling and sending and researching. Thank you to David K. Abraham for consistently sharing a different perspective from that of my team.

I have Rachel Boxman to thank for compiling the blogs and getting them ready for printing. I met Rachel through the blogs. She was a reader of the blogs, then a responder, and now a colleague and friend.

I want to thank Bill, Josh, Jeffrey, and Katie for being frequent subjects of the blogs. They have allowed me to write about them and share their stories long after they were old enough to read the stories and know about them. Most family members want their wife or mother to succeed, but most would prefer that their wife or mother succeed without speaking and writing about them! Thank you to my family for being supportive of this part of my work. You have each been quite generous.

Additional thanks to Katie for starting the compilation process and saying, "Mom, some of these are good." The ultimate compliment. And extra thanks for Bill who reads every blog before it goes out and reminds me to get permission if I am using real names. His protection of my relationship means I still have relationships.

Please know that all the stories are true. If the blog pertains to one of my clients, the names have been changed. If the blog is about a family member, I have their permission.

And thanks most of all to my clients. I appreciate your trust and your willingness to open your work and personal lives with me. You are each so important to me and you complete the mosaic of my life. Without you I would have nothing to write about and no way to pursue my passion! I might have to go out and eat worms!

Made in the USA
Middletown, DE
17 February 2019